KU-132-993

THE IMPERIAL WAY

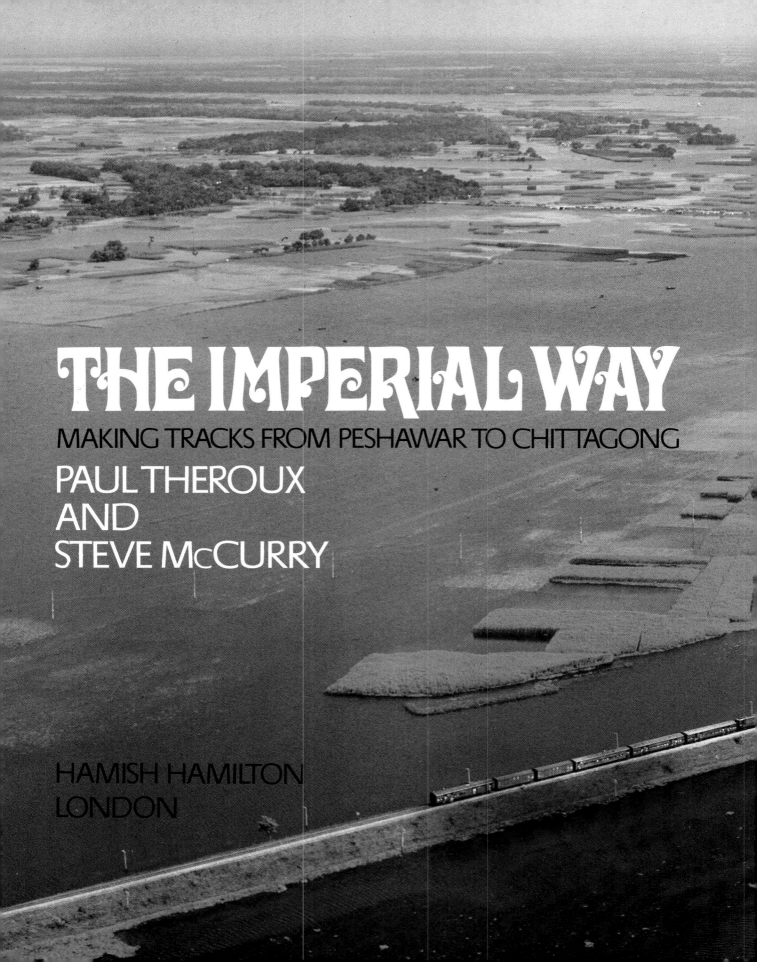

THE IMPERIAL WAY

MAKING TRACKS FROM PESHAWAR TO CHITTAGONG

PAUL THEROUX
AND
STEVE McCURRY

HAMISH HAMILTON
LONDON

First published in Great Britain 1985
by Hamish Hamilton Ltd
Garden House 57–59 Long Acre London WC2E 9JZ

Text copyright © 1985 by Cape Cod Scriveners Co.
All photographs are copyright © Steve McCurry except those on the
following pages: 33, 36, 37, 38, 39, 52–53, 54–55, 56 (left), 57, 58,
59, 65, 68–69, 72–73, 74–75, 76, 78–79, 80, 81, 82–83, 85, 88,
90–91, 93, 98–99, 101, 104, 107, 108–109, 114–115, 122–123,
126–127, 132–133, 136–137, jacket front and back, which are
copyright © National Geographic Society.

Photographs edited by Lauren Stockbower

Maps drawn by Robin Jacques

Book design by Gerald Cinamon

British Library Cataloguing in Publication Data

Theroux, Paul
The imperial way : making tracks from Peshawar
to Chittagong.
1. Railroads——India   2. India——Description and travel——1947–1980
I. Title   II. McCurry, Steve
915.4′0452   DS414

ISBN 0-241-11668-6

Typeset in Monophoto Photina by
MS Filmsetting Limited, Frome
Printed and bound in Italy by
Arnoldo Mondadori Editore, Verona

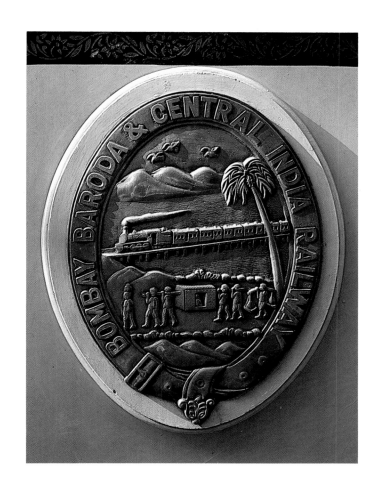

PAKISTAN

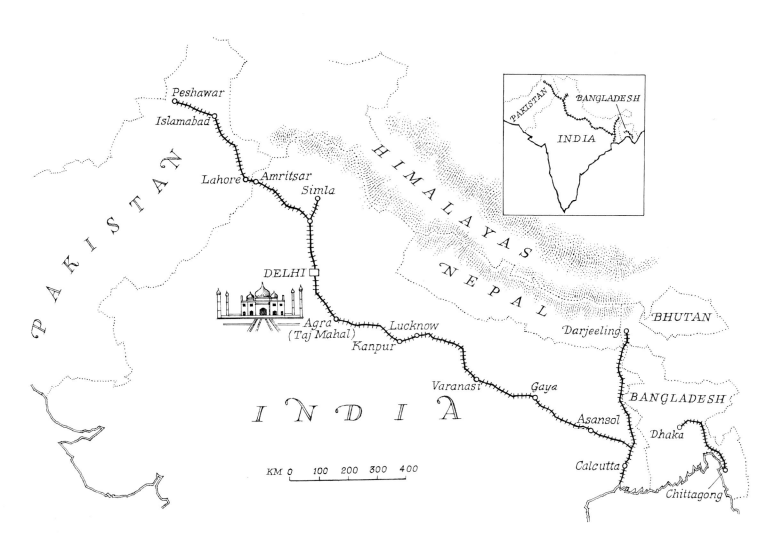

INTRODUCTION BY PAUL THEROUX

THE KHYBER RAILWAY

"This is the Qissa Khawani Bazaar," said Ziarat Gul in Peshawar. Mr. Gul was a powerfully-built and kindly soul who was known locally as "Gujjar" – "Buffalo Man". He was pointing at a labyrinth of alleys too narrow for anything but pony carts.

"It means 'The Storytellers' Bazaar'. In the old times all the *kafilas* (caravans) came from Persia and Russia and Afghanistan, here to Peshawar. They told stories of their journeys."

But Peshawar is once again a great destination. Now the travellers are Afghan refugees and the stories in the bazaar concern the heroism of Pathans ambushing Russian convoys. Peshawar had always struck me as the most old-fashioned, the most traditional and, in many respects, one of the most unchanged towns of the British Raj. This flavour today is even stronger, as the gun-toting tribal people leave their rocky villages and mud huts and troop through the Khyber Pass to shelter here in Pakistan. There are said to be more than a million of them, and many of them bring goods and food to sell at the bazaar – carpets and jewelry, embroidery, leatherwork, cartridge belts, pistol holsters, rifle slings, almonds, dates, prunes, and fresh fruit. The bazaar has never been busier or more full of hawkers, and everywhere are the beaky craggy faces of the travellers, the turbanned men and shrouded women, the rifles and pistols, and the tea-drinkers huddled around samovars – storytellers again.

And still, once a week, the Khyber Railway descends the 3500 feet from the highest point of the Khyber Pass, carrying the refugees and travellers who can afford the seven rupee train fare. It is one of the most atmospheric railways in the Sub-continent, and it is because it is required to climb such steep inclines that it is powered by two steam engines – one at the front and one at the rear of the five coaches – both belching smoke and whistling as the little train makes the journey to and from Landi Kotal.

I had not been here for ten years, but I had happy memories of these railways. And so I decided to trace a line from Peshawar to Chittagong and take all the trains that lay in between. It was to be neither a vacation nor an ordeal, but rather a kind of sedentary adventuring – an imperial progress along the railways of the old Raj.

I started from Jamrud, a deserted station, a short distance from Jamrud Fort which, having been built in 1836, is just ninety years older than the Khyber Railway. It was an early morning in July, and very hot – the monsoon was weeks overdue.

"Once there was no trouble here," a man told me on the train as we clattered across the plain. "There was no water, no trees. Only small villages. Then a dam was built and water came to the valley in a stream, and since then there has been constant fighting."

There were thirty policemen standing in the sun at various distances along the stream. I learned later that there had been a local squabble over the land – it was irrigated and now valuable; ten men had been killed in the quarrel and the police were trying to pacify the opposing families.

Tempers were very bad: the months of drought had scorched the face of the land and made it so hot that people had moved out of their houses and set up their string beds under trees – I counted fourteen beds under the dusty leaves of one large tree. To cool themselves, men sat on the banks of the stream trickling beside the railway tracks and they chatted keeping their feet in the water.

There were over thirty-five thousand people in the Kacha Garhi Refugee Camp, and nearly as many in the one at Nasir Bagh not far away. They lay in hammocks, they cooked under trees, they waited for the daily shipment of food; they watched the train go by.

Across the ten miles of gravel are the high grey-brown mountains which mark the border of Afghanistan, and the black smoking train makes its way across the dead land.

It is perhaps the best way to begin the long railway journey on the imperial route through Pakistan and across the top of India to Bangladesh, to the end of the line at Chittagong. It is the best way because nothing has changed on this railway for over one hundred and fifty years. This was always a tribal area, the people were always dressed like this, and always armed, the train was always powered by smoking screeching steam engines, and the night-time noises were always human voices and the clopping hooves of the tonga ponies, and when – hours late – the train pulls into Peshawar Cantonment Station, the passengers hurry in various directions – to "Lower Class Exit" or "First Class Exit," to "Woman's Waiting Room" or "Waiting Room for Gents." It is pitch dark and a hundred and ten degrees. As in the old days most people make straight for the Storytellers' Bazaar.

I went from Peshawar Station to the hotel for a beer. Because of the new and fervent Islamic policies, I was asked to sign a form in quadruplicate, giving my name, my father's name and various dates and addresses – it was like a scholarship form – and, when this was approved and countersigned and stamped, I was led to the empty and rather sordid Permit Room of Dean's Hotel where, for much more than it was worth, I was sold a bottle of beer. The Drinking Permit with all the signatures and stamps, incriminated and shamed me. After that I drank soda pop for the sake of my dignity.

THE KHYBER MAIL

Ten years ago I had come to Peshawar and asked for a bedroll for the train and was told they had none. This evening I inquired again and was told they had one – but only one: "You may book it." I gladly did so and then stood with it under a whirring fan. Most of the larger railway stations in Pakistan and India have ceiling fans on the outdoor platforms, which is why the people waiting are spaced so evenly – clustered in little groups at regular intervals. The humming fans make one feel one is trapped in a food processor.

It was an air-conditioned compartment and in its grumbling way the machinery actually worked. I was soon travelling under a bright moon through Nowshera and across the Indus River at Attock on its hundred-year-old bridge. We passed through Rawalpindi and Jhelum, too, but by then I was asleep.

Just before Wazirabad at dawn there was a knock on the door of my compartment.

"You wanting breakfast?"

I could have been wrong of course, but it seemed to be the same brisk man who had asked the question ten years ago: it was the same bad eye, the same dirty turban, the same lined face. And the breakfast was the same – eggs, tea, bread on heavy stained crockery.

I did not think it was a coincidence. I had returned to take this long trip again to see what had changed. I had noticed very few changes. Pakistan was more Islamic, and the crowds were denser, but what else was different? Very little; and more interestingly, the same people seemed to be running things – driving trains, selling tickets, making breakfasts and punching tickets. The reason was that people who run railways tend to have the job for life and to take it fairly seriously. The railway is one of the most traditional of institutions and, for better or worse, it runs in Pakistan pretty much the same as it always ran. It has not really been modernized, but you get the idea that even moderniz-ation wouldn't change it very much. The odd thing is that throughout the Sub-continent the railway seems so profoundly part of the culture that it hardly seems related to the industrial age but instead seems as ancient as India itself. The roads and airports come and go, but nothing seems so indestructible as the railway. And throughout most of my travels I thought: if it were not for the railway nothing would work, no one would travel, no business would be done and no people would be fed. It is a permanent fixture – part of the culture because it is part of the land, as natural as a gully or a hill.

There was evidence that some scattered showers of the monsoon had reached the outskirts of Lahore, now the capital of Punjab. It was cooler here and the rice fields had water in them; planting had begun; the grass was green. There had been no grass anywhere on the Frontier. Here the soil was mostly clay and so brickworks had sprung up, each one with a steeple-like chimney. Little girls, some looking as young as six or seven, were digging mud and clay out of pits for bricks and carrying it in baskets on their heads. In sharp contrast to this, little boys were playing gaily in the grass or else swimming in ditches. It is the absurd puritanism of the country that requires little girls modestly to remain clothed and do laborious work, while naked boys can frolic all the livelong day.

Nearer Shahdara Bagh there was luminous green slime on some pools and others were choked with water hyacinths, and there was a slum village of wickerwork houses next to the Ravi Bridge. The decrepitude was interesting because not far from Shahdara Station is one of Pakistan's most glorious buildings, the Tomb of Jahangir, with its vast park – grander than the Shalimar Gardens – and the marble mausoleum inlaid with gems; all of it in a perfect state of preservation. It is one of the noblest Moghul structures, and not even Lahore Fort, or the immense and crumbling Anarkali Bazaar, or the Badshahi Mosque – largest in the world – can compare with its gentle beauty. Surrounded by palms, it lies outside Lahore, another marvel on the north-west railway.

THE INTERNATIONAL EXPRESS: THE 208 DOWN TO INDIA

When India was partitioned in 1947, so was the railway, but the trains did not stop running until the 1965 Indo-Pakistani war. The tracks were not removed, and though there were no trains the steel rails still connected Wagha in Pakistan with Atari, the Indian border town. And then in 1976 the trains began to run again. Very little had changed on this line: the steam locomotives, like all steam locomotives in India, looked filthy, ancient, and reliable; they are great sooty thunder boxes, and there are 7,245 of them still operating in India; and the travellers no matter what their religion or nationality still privately celebrated the fact that they were Punjabis. The coaches were battered, and the train was very slow. This was the International Express.

"Too late," the policeman said, grinning at me from behind the gate at Lahore Station. It was ten past eight, the train was scheduled to leave at nine. "It is closed."

"Open the gate," I said, showing him my tickets.

He hesitated. His expression changed to one of disappointment, and glumly he opened the gate and let me through, so that I could catch the train.

The Customs and Immigration bottlenecks were set up there at Lahore Station – platform one – and four officials, one after the other, peered at me and said, "Profession?" I said I was a writer. "Ah, books."

I said, "Shall I open my suitcase?"

"As you wish."

Standing on the platform I realized that Pakistan now seemed a more Muslim society, and so more masculine. More women wore shrouds or veils, and the men had acquired a sort of swagger, and stared at foreigners and looked indifferent and disapproving and covetous at the same time.

The train left on time, which surprised me, considering that the thousand or so people on board had all had their passports stamped and their luggage examined. We travelled across a plain towards India. After an hour every man we passed had acquired a turban. We were nearing Amritsar, spiritual capital of the Sikhs, and we were among the great family of Singhs, with their strange light eyes and long hair. Sikh is from the Sanskrit word *shishya*, meaning "disciple". The Sikhs are disciples of a tradition of ten gurus, beginning with the sixteenth-century Guru Nanak who taught monotheism, espoused meditation, and opposed the Hindu caste system. On the approaches to Amritsar, Sikhs herded goats, Sikhs dug in the fields, Sikhs processed the passengers on the International Express. This was Atari Station and the operation took several hours: everyone ordered off the train, everyone lined up and scrutinized, everyone ordered back on. Then the whistle blew and the black smoke darkened the sky, and we proceeded into India.

But it was not only black smoke in the sky. The clouds were the colour of cast iron; they were blue-black and huge. I had never in my life seen such ominous clouds. It is usually possible in India to tell whether it will rain from the whiteness of the egrets – they look whitest when rain is due; and these dozens flying up from the rice paddies near Amritsar were brilliantly white against the dark clouds massing over us.

We arrived just before one o'clock at Amritsar, and as we pulled in, passing buffaloes and scattering the goats and ducks and children, the storm hit. It was the first rain of the monsoon – pelting grey drops, noisy and powerful and already, only minutes after it had begun, erupting from drains and streaming under the tracks. It was coming down so hard I had to shout to be heard at the Enquiry Window – I was making an onward reservation. No one left the station. What was the point? It was a ceaseless cataract which had flooded the station car park. And the passengers from the International Express steamed as they looked through the station arches, and they marvelled at the monsoon – the first rain to hit the city in months. The rain in its fury put the Indians into a good mood. It was the sunny days and blue skies that made them bad-tempered.

They needed some smiles in Amritsar. There had recently been riots and political killings, and on most days a man stood outside the Golden Temple – sacred to the Sikhs – and chanted against the government, while scores of policemen waited anxiously in nearby doorways. A large number of Sikhs were agitating for a Free Punjab and for Amritsar to be designated a Holy City (like Varanasi and Hardwar). It was not so much secession as some Sikhs demanding to be regarded as a separate race rather than religious followers.

Because of the rain, only rickshaws were running in Amritsar. Cars lay stranded and submerged all over the inundated city. I sat inside, deafened by the rain, and studied the Indian Railway Timetable, and after a while I became curious about the route of a certain train out of Amritsar. This particular mail train left Amritsar at ten in the evening and headed south of the main line to Delhi; but halfway there it made a hairpin turn at Ambala and raced north to Kalka where, at dawn, it connected with the railcar to Simla. It was an extraordinary route – and a very fast train: instead of going to bed in the hotel, I could reserve a sleeper, and board the train, and more or less wake up in the foothills of the Himalayas, in Simla.

THE SIMLA MAIL

Amritsar was under water, and apart from the rickshaws gurgling slowly through the flooded streets, the only movement in the city was at the railway station. Trains were coming and going, and the lights in the station yard made a strange Venetian water-glow of swimming flares among the flooded tracks. But it had now stopped raining, and the night air was clear and cool.

It was not a popular train, this Simla Mail. It was an odd twisted route that took us east to Jullundur and then south to Ludhiana and then sharply to the north-east, to Chandigarh, Kalka and finally due north to Simla. It was an old route and, undoubtedly, the result of the imperial postal service, for the British regarded letter writing and mail delivery as one of the distinguishing features of any great civilization. And Indians have pretty much subscribed to the paper theory of civilization – even an application for a five rupee bedroll is done in triplicate.

The train was fascinating but filthy. It is often the case in India. The sleeping compartment had not been swept; it was small, badly painted and dirty, with barred windows and a steel door.

"Use the shutters," the ticket collector said, "and don't leave any small articles lying around."

The whistle of the Simla Mail drowned the sounds of music from the bazaar and the howls of Sikh agitators who were attracting crowds just outside the station. It was 9.50 at night and I was soon asleep. But at midnight I was woken by rain beating against the shutters. The monsoon which had hit the Punjab only the day before had brought another storm, and the train struggled through it. The thick raindrops came down so hard they spattered through the slats and louvres in the shutters and a fine spray soaked the compartment floor.

The Guard knocked on the door at Kalka at 5.20 to announce that we had arrived. It is the custom to tip the Guard, and so I did: "I have a tip for you. Keep your sleeping compartments clean and your passengers will be much happier."

It was cool and green at Kalka, and after a shave in the Gentlemen's Waiting Room I was ready for the five-hour journey through the hills to Simla. I could have taken the small pottering "Simla Queen" or the express, but the white twenty-seat railcar was already waiting at the platform. I boarded, and snoozed, and woke to see mists lying across the hills and heavy green foliage in the glades beside the line.

Two hours later at 5,000 feet we came to the little station at Barog, where every day the railcar waits while the passengers have breakfast; and then it sets off again into the low tumbling cloud. Occasionally the cloud and mist was broken by a shaft of light and it parted to reveal a valley floor thousands of feet below.

Solan Brewery, on the line to Simla, is both a brewery and a railway station. But the station came afterwards, for the brewery was started in the nineteenth century by a British company which found good spring water here in these hills of Himachal Pradesh. In 1904, when the railway was built, the line was cut right through the brewery. All the trains become filled with the rich smell of malt and hops as they approach this station.

The Company Secretary, Mr. H. N. Handa, told me that business was excellent and, indeed, sales are increasing.

"But we have known difficult times," he said. "Our darkest days were during the Morarji Desai government. He introduced prohibition. We thought we were finished! And yet we managed quite well."

I asked him how.

He said, "We started to bottle mineral water. It sold wonderfully. It is highly recommended by Doctor Wilhelm Schnieder. His chemical analysis is given on the label."

As I travelled on I thought of how, ten years ago, I had been here on this train and seen the same signs near the flowers at Barog – "No Plucking," and had the same breakfast at the same hour, and seen the same pious mottoes on the walls at Solan Brewery, and at noon Simla was the same collection of bungalows and mansions. Nothing, it seemed, had changed; or was this one of the illusions of riding the railway?

Motor vehicles are banned from most of Simla's roads, and so nearly everyone in Simla is a pedestrian, glad for the chance to wear tweed suits and sweaters and to stroll in the thick fog. When it rained in Simla, as it did often at this time of year, water spouted from the eaves of houses and it flooded the gutters in the road, and it washed across the whole town – wetting the blacksmiths and flower-sellers, the spice traders and vegetable barrows, soaking the awnings and the heavy tread of Tibetans tramping with sacks of coal on their back, and the song of the tall old man playing his flute in the rain and wearing a red tin sign saying that he is blind.

It is the opinion of the Indian in the hill station that the plains are disorderly and crime-ridden. It may be merely a conceit, but it is a very common one, the belief that as soon as they are above three or four thousand feet people tend to behave themselves. "People on the plains indulge in bad behaviour, indiscipline and mischief," a man at Simla station told me. He was a train Guard, but he was full of complaints about vandalism and tardiness and "mischief – especially political mischief."

"You're very frank, sir," I said.

"It is because I have resigned," he replied. "I gave in my notice two months ago. I am not sorry. When I started working in 1944 a man was reprimanded if he turned up late. I was once three minutes' late and it was a serious matter. Now it is nothing. But if a man is late how can he ask others to be on time?"

The residents of Simla are often visited by relatives. "They always say, 'I'm coming for two or three days,' but after three weeks they're still here. And there is something about this air that excites them and makes them difficult."

The man speaking was an army colonel. His English was perfect. He said that he had been taught by Irish priests in Musoorie. "It is a characteristic of the Irish," he said, "that they do not pass on their accent."

The colonel had a remedy for unwelcome guests. He made lists of sights that were not to be missed in Simla. Each one was a day's walk from his house and it was usually at the top of a steep hill. After a few days of this sightseeing the starch was taken out of his guests and they were fairly glad when it was time to go.

I said, "A military solution?"

"Just so," he said.

The most knowledgeable railway buff I met in Simla was a man who, over a period of years, had travelled all over India on trains visiting race tracks. He seldom stayed overnight. He would hurry to Lucknow on a night train, gamble all day at the track, and then catch the sleeper to Calcutta and do the same thing. He had been from Peshawar to Madras, from one race meeting to another. I said it seemed a difficult thing to do, all that railroading. No, he said, the difficult thing was putting on a sad face and hailing a tonga and then riding Third Class so that no one would guess that he had five thousand rupees of winnings in his pocket.

THE TWO-DOWN TO DELHI

At their best the Indian trains are more than comfortable – they are actually cozy. I glided down from Simla in the little blue train to Kalka and then in the late evening boarded the sleeper for Delhi. It was air-conditioned, it was clean, and the bed was made – starched sheets and a soft pillow. There was no better way to Delhi. All night my dreams were full of the gentle rumble of the train crossing the province of Haryana, and at seven the next morning I looked out the window and saw the outskirts of Delhi, now grey and sodden in the rain.

India is peculiarly visible from a railway train. I have the idea that much of Indian life is lived within sight of he tracks or the station, and often next to the tracks, or inside the station. It is as if Indians still associate the railway with progress and optimism – certainly, in India, the railway represents prosperity, and few ambitions could be realized without it. It is not only part of Indian culture, but it is an ingredient in Indian life: it is dynamic, energetic, powerful. Why else would so many people choose to live so close to it? And so merely by sitting at a window seat and watching, one gets a very full idea of Indian society. But it is also true to say that Indians keep themselves near the tracks in order to watch the trains go by, so that they can see how other people live.

Some men in Delhi who were members of an offshoot of the official railway union were holding a hunger strike at the residence of the Minister of Railways. I had seen the union's posters in Simla – "*Inkalab Jindabad!*" was printed in red: "Long Live Revolution!" I found the forty men camped outside the minister's wall. The leader, Mr. Sharma, had not eaten anything for four days ("Just some salted water and some lime water"). He said, "Have you any questions to ask me?"

"Yes. I'm curious to know whether you're hungry."

"I am not hungry, but I feel weak," he said. He said he planned to starve himself for a few more days and then, if the minister would not listen to his grievances, he would consider more action. Then he went back to sleep as the men chanted the practically unchantable name of their union. "All-India Shunting Cabin and Traffic Staff Association," they chanted, and then they too went to sleep.

But the strikers were relatively few in number, and over at Old Delhi Station the trains were running normally. It seemed to me that the unluckiest railwayman in this season of withering heat was a fireman on a steam locomotive. Rambling around the station yard I discovered an even more exhausting job: boilermaker. The boilermaker is essentially a welder, but because he deals with all aspects of the boiler he is often required to crawl inside the boiler or the firebox and use his welding torch in this confined space. Today it was 103° at the Old Delhi loco shed, but Suresh Baboo, a boilermaker, crawled out of a locomotive's firebox to tell me that he was not deterred by a little thing like heat.

I was curious about his salary for this difficult job. He was a railwayman Grade Two and earned one thousand rupees a month (£100) of which four hundred was his "Dearness Allowance" ("Because in Delhi, food and living are very dear").

Was this enough to live on? I wondered. He said no, not in Delhi. "We are asking for an increase in the Dearness."

"And by the by," he said, "my name is not really Suresh Baboo. That is the name I put down on my paper when I did my Matric. I am a Christian. My name is Samuel – "

"For some reason – probably because of the British tradition – morale among railwaymen is very high," said Mr. K. T. V. Raghavan, Chairman of the Indian Railway Board. His position in the hierarchy of the Indian Civil Service shows the importance of the railway in India: he is the second most senior civil servant in the country. He said that the splinter unions represented no more than twenty to twenty-five percent of the work force, and that there hadn't been a serious strike for almost ten years. "A railway strike is unnecessary, because we can sort out our differences across the table."

Mr. Raghavan impressed me by speaking of the special nature of the railway in India. It was not merely a way of going to and from work, but rather in India a solution to the complex demands of the family. Birth, death, marriage, illness, and religious festivals all required witnesses and rituals which implied a journey home. Indians, Mr. Raghavan said, only *seemed* restless travellers; in fact, most of them were merely showing piety and carrying out religious or domestic duties.

The statistics associated with Indian Railways are elephantine (ten million passengers a day, eleven thousand trains, almost two million workers, and so forth), but the memorable details are simple enough: it is self-sufficient in rolling stock – India manufactures all her own coaches and engines – and it makes an operating profit of twelve percent revenue over expenditure. In many respects, India is the world's greatest railway nation – the most trains, the most passengers, the longest system, the most stations; and also in a negative sense – the most cockroaches, the greatest number of rats living under railway platforms, the most forms to fill out, and some of the dirtiest sleeping cars.

"We know all this," Mr. Raghavan said. "Our priorities now are to provide a more efficient, cleaner, faster service for the passenger. We need to do more, and we're doing it – slowly. My concern is for the travelling public. And I am determined to keep rail fares as low as possible, so that the poorest people can still travel."

In the succeeding days I buttonholed railway passengers and asked them what they thought of the service. The most common complaint was that trains were unpunctual – few people mentioned poor food, dirty coaches or cows roaming the railway platforms.

It was in Delhi that I found the best organized railway station in India. This was Hazrat Nizamuddin Station, just south of the city and a short walk from Humayun's Tomb – which is reddish and swollen and was the prototype for the Taj Mahal.

There were no cows, no rats, no three-legged dogs at Hazrat Nizamuddin Station; instead there were flowers and shrubs in pots on the platform, and every day on the orders of the stationmaster, Mr. G. L. Suri, ant powder was sprinkled along the walls.

"See? No papers. No flies. Look at the Ladies' Waiting Room – look at the floors!" Mr. Suri proudly took me on a tour of the station. He hadn't been recommended to me by the Railway Board – I had simply stopped on one of the one hundred and eighty trains that pass through each day and noticed how unusual it looked. "Look at my catering facilities – come into my kitchen."

How was it possible to keep a station so clean in the hot season?

Mr. Suri said, "I do my duty – I get satisfaction from it. Sometimes I work sixteen hours a day. I do not accept excuses." He nodded and added softly, "And I am very tough."

THE JANATA-MADRAS EXPRESS, TO AGRA

The Janata–Madras Express passes through Hazrat Nizamuddin Station, and of course it stops, because "Janata" means "People" and the People's Express stops everywhere. It is probably the slowest express in the world. I met a man on it who was going to Nagpur. "I will be in Nagpur tomorrow afternoon, or maybe evening – or perhaps night – "

But he faced the prospect of twenty-four hours on a wooden seat with

Indian patience. "I will eat some fruits, I will rest my body, I will read some literature..."

It would be several days before this long rumbling steam train arrived in Madras. It was cheap – all second class – but it was not really for long-distance passengers; it went fifteen hundred miles, stopping at every station – just like a country bus – and most people only went a few miles.

It was easy to tell the long-distance travellers. In India, they are heavily laden, and always carry a big steel trunk. At railway stations in India one sees the family grouped around the trunk – they sit on it, sleep beside it, use it for a table, and when their train draws in they hire a skinny man to wrestle it on board.

I met a man on the Janata–Madras Express who told me what was inside these trunks.

"My mother was typical," he said. "She carried all her jewellery and all her saris – thirty or forty of them. She brought glasses to drink out of, cooking utensils, plates and the trays we call *thali*. She took the essential household. All Indians do this. The trouble was that my mother used to take all these things even if she was only going away for a day or so – but I broke her of that habit..."

It seemed that the trunk was an Indian's best defence against being robbed, contaminated or stranded: it made them completely portable and very safe. At any moment, using the trunk, an Indian could set up house.

"You should have caught the Taj Express," the Guard said as he punched my ticket. "It is very fast and clean..."

His implication was that the Janata Express was slow and dirty – and it *was* slow and dirty. The coaches looked frightful – they were dark, dusty with the soot of the steam engine, and very crowded. But the filth was inevitable on such a train – so crowded, and with all the windows open – and the people were gentle.

"You're not going far," I was reminded.

No, only to Agra – six hours on this slow beast; but six hours was nothing on an Indian train, where some people might say, "When do I arrive? Let me see. Today is Thursday and tomorrow is..."

I was sitting across from Bansilal Bajaj, who was on Home Leave from Abu Dhabi – every two years he got two months' leave, and he spent a month of that on Indian Railways, going up and down the country. He had just come from Hardwar. He too was on his way to Agra.

"In Abu Dhabi all we do is work. I am in the catering and cleaning business, but I am no more than a machine. When I come back to India I am human again."

It was a lovely evening, very clear, just after a heavy rainstorm of the monsoon. Now there was not a cloud in the sky, and in the west it was the colour of a tropical sea – greeny-blue, reflected in perfectly still pools and paddy fields. Not a breath of wind in this waterworld, and the palms were flat and dark, like cut-outs. There was a sweetness in the air and for a number of miles no people – just colour and empty space and darting birds.

Just after dark the lights in the train failed, and we travelled clattering through pitch-blackness, with the steam engine puffing and wheezing, and the whistle blowing off-key, and the only lights were the sparks from the smokestack, sailing past the window like fireflies.

It was almost nine by the time we arrived in Agra. The town is nothing. The Agra Fort is substantial, Akbar's Mausoleum of Sikandra has character, and the Moti Masjid (the "Pearl Mosque") has person ality; but the Taj Mahal is something else. It hardly matters that it is so difficult to describe, because just looking at it you are certain that you will never forget it. It is not merely a visual experience, but an emotional one – its pure symmetry imparts such strong feeling; and it is a spiritual experience, too; for the Taj Mahal is alone among buildings I have seen. It is not merely lovely; it looks as if it has a soul.

THE GANGA-YAMUNA EXPRESS TO VARANASI

It was after eleven at night, and very hot, and the dust stirred all day by the humans and their animals was just beginning to settle. It was a good time for boarding a train and leaving town – but not any old train. The Ganga–Yamuna Express was any old train. Even First Class was dirty; there was no bedding; the fans were broken – and, when I left the shutters open for the breeze, hot cinders blew through the window and fouled the compartment. There was no food, no water; the seats were torn. It was like a certain kind of Asiatic prison cell.

It was a long night. Dawn broke at Kanpur, and two hours later at Lucknow it was very sunny and bright, a noontime heat, though it was hardly half-past seven in the morning. After the village of Safdarganj there were great green fields – the meadowy illusion of rice growing in geometric pools of mud. This is the Gangetic plain – very fertile between here and Varanasi, and especially this month, as the rains had just begun and all the paddy fields were brim full. The rains were dangerously strong in Hardwar and had flooded Delhi, but here beside the line of the Ganga–Yamuna Express they had guaranteed a great rice crop and had given the landscape the serene look of a Daniell aquatint – the palms very still, the buffaloes obedient, the Indians up to their shins in water, and an almost emblematic mother weeding vegetables with

19

her infant in the middle of another field under the shade of a big black umbrella.

Rice is a tedious and complicated crop, and a good harvest depends as much on meteorological luck as on hard work; but for miles, for hours – for days on these plains – you see nothing else at this time of year: men, women and children planting, or ploughing or tending the crop, and all of them working under the blazing sun and burned as black as their buffaloes.

The passing train excites the birds. There are three birds that are never out of view in India: the House Crow – an oversize busybody; the Common Myna – noisy and adaptable; and the Pariah Kite – greedily watchful. These three birds do more than the Ministry of Works to tidy up the Sub-continent. There are others, too – brighter or more feathery – the white Little Egret, the rose-ringed parakeet, the collared dove, the kingfisher, and the nimble black drongo which chases insects like a stunt flier.

The villages were small – mud huts and grass roofs, like a glimpse of central Africa in Uttar Pradesh, except that in the centre of the frail village was always a substantial stone temple. Most of these villages were nameless, but sometimes a tiny station or a halt displayed the name. One sun-baked station in the middle of the hot plain was Rudanli. Three horse-drawn tongas were waiting at the platform, and some people looked hopefully up from their tin trunks. But the Ganga–Yamuna Express did not stop.

We were going the long way to Varanasi, taking "the Faizabad Loop," via Ayodhya where the monkeys on the platform sat on the ink-blots of shade. We passed through Shahganj, where rice planters stood scanning the blue sky for clouds; and then after Jaunpur we joined the main line.

Varanasi Station has the contours of a Hindu temple, built in the Mauryan style, and like a temple it is filled with holy men and pilgrims. It is also full of sacred cows. The cows at Varanasi station are wise to the place – they get water at the drinking fountains, food near the refreshment stalls, shelter along the platforms, and exercise beside the tracks; they also know how to use the cross-over bridges and can climb up and down the steepest stairs.

"We are installing cow-catchers," the Station Superintendent told me – but he did not mean the traditional ones, on the engines, he meant fences to prevent the cows from entering the station.

The flocks of goats at Varanasi Station are on their way to the Ganges to have their throats cut and be dumped into the river as a sacrifice; the beggars are testing the piety of the pilgrims; and those small narrow bundles that are part of so many of the travellers' luggage are in fact human corpses, headed for the cremation fires on the ghats. Varanasi is the essential India: stinks and perfumes; and because nothing that is holy in India can be regarded as dirty it is one of the filthiest of Indian cities and positively stinking with sanctity. I met an Indian medical student who had just arrived in Varanasi. He was on his way to the Ganges to take his ritual bath. He said he was definitely planning to bathe in the Ganges, among the corpses of goats and monkeys and corpses of dead beggars who died at the station and were taken in rickshaws to the river and thrown in uncremated.

"Oh, yes," the medical student said. "I will immerse myself."

"What about the health aspect?"

He said, "It is a question of mind over matter."

But it was not the only contradiction I saw in Varanasi. Nailed to a wall that was smeared with betel juice was the sign SPITTING IN PUBLIC IS INJURIOUS TO HEALTH. Most signs in railway stations seemed rather futile; it seemed to be part of their charm. DISCIPLINE MAKES THE NATION GREAT and SPEED THRILLS BUT ALSO KILLS and BE INDIAN, BUY INDIAN and SMALL FAMILY, HAPPY FAMILY.

And Varanasi Station made me think how closely it resembled its city. Indeed, every Indian railway station accurately represented its town or city – it was just as small or large or clean or dirty or smug or desperate. Every airport in the world is practically identical – like a branch of the same unimaginative corporation or chain store. But every railway station is different and unique. When you get off a train and enter the station you know exactly where you are.

THE HOWRAH MAIL

Howrah Station in Calcutta is the clearest proof of that. The Howrah Mail, one of India's best trains, leaves Varanasi at 5.30 in the morning, just as the passengers from Delhi are yawning and peering out the window and getting their first glimpses of the holy city. And the people waiting on the platform at Varanasi are watching the train with admiration, because this train represents luxury – it has three Chair Cars, and sleeping cars, and a Pantry Car, where food is cooked and dished up in trays which are distributed around the train by waiters. The Howrah Mail is efficiently air-conditioned; it is famous for being fast and is nearly always on time.

Today it was slightly late, because there was a drama at Mogulsarai Junction. A woman woke up in one of the Chair Cars and saw that her suitcase had been stolen from the overhead rack. She screamed and yanked the Alarm Chain and brought the speeding train to a halt. The police were summoned. The woman made a statement itemizing the contents of her suitcase – her monologue took thirty minutes – and then we were on our way.

From a distance in the early morning, Varanasi looks wonderful, and the most glorious sight of it is from the Howrah Mail as it crosses the Dufferin Bridge which spans the Ganges just east of the city. From this high vantage point the whole populous riverbank and all the ghats can be seen gilded in the light of the rising sun, and its splendour is intensified because the distance hides the city's decay, and at this time of day – the early morning – the river is filled with people washing, praying, swimming and generally doing their *puja*. One gets a very good idea of the size and sprawl of Varanasi, which is greatly in contrast with the opposite bank, nearly empty except for the fort at Ramnagur to the west, which is still the residence of the Maharaja of Benares.

From here – the outskirts of Varanasi all the way to Calcutta – the land is waterlogged and fertile, an endless rice field. But this railway line crosses a number of great landmarks. A few hours after leaving Varanasi we were crossing the Son River on the fourth longest bridge in the world; and farther on, at Sasaram, you can look out of the window of the train and see the red stone mausoleum of Sher Shah, who ruled Delhi in the sixteenth century; and at noon the train stops at Gaya, where Buddha received enlightenment.

Gaya also marks the beginning of a very strange landscape. Sudden single hills are thrust out of the flatness like massive dinosaurs petrified on the flat plain; and other hills are like pyramids, and still more like slag heaps. They stand alone, these odd shapes, and though at Gaya they have temples and ruins on their summits, farther on they are barren, with only a few trees or a small village at their base. They don't seem to belong to any range of hills and have a comic plopped-down look.

At Koderma, the land glitters – it really sparkles: the roads are spangled and the train-yards are full of sequins. It is mica, which is mined nearby, and either it has been spilled or else the land is full of mica chips. And then the landscape changes again and becomes like the setting for Kipling's "The Strange Ride of Morrowbie Jukes" – complete with gullies, and craters, and scavenging crows.

We had been travelling through Bihar, but at the town of Dhanbad we came to West Bengal. It was wet and cool and jungly here, and when the train stopped some blind beggars got on. The Ticket Examiner asked them to beg in a different part of the train and they meekly agreed.

This Ticket Examiner was a woman – one of three or four women who work on the Howrah Mail. "And there are many women working in the railway. Just because you haven't seen them personally doesn't mean that they aren't there," she said.

Her name was Ollie Francis. "I was a Christian," she said. "But then

I married Mr. Ningam and so I became a Hindu. For the children's sake. It would have been too confusing for them otherwise. It was not an arranged marriage. I married for love.''

She had seven children, the eldest eighteen, the youngest five. She missed them when she made this Calcutta run, but her relatives helped look after them. She had worked for the railways for twenty years. She said she enjoyed her work – "And there are also financial considerations.''

What Ollie liked best about the Howrah Mail was its speed – less than fourteen hours from Varanasi to Calcutta. As the train drew into Howrah at seven o'clock the daylight was extinguished by smoke, and rain mixed with fog; frightening numbers of people were making their way through the mud and the lamplight. It had been a very long day; and almost the first thing I saw at the station was a completely naked man crying and screaming "No! No!'' and backing away as a policeman smacked him with a wooden stave. The naked man sort of bumped past me at the ticket barrier and then moved on, with the policeman after him, as a crowd gathered to watch.

But of course Howrah is Calcutta: the elegant ticket windows, all glass and carvings, are one of the finest examples of railway architecture in India; and the opposite of elegance – distress and destitution, beggars and animals and idle mobs that look so starved you might take them for predators. And Howrah is very large; but also like Calcutta it is in a state of decay. Enormous and noisy, a combination of grandeur and desolation, the wonder is that it still works.

I am fascinated by Calcutta. It is one of the cities of the world that I associate with the future. This is how New York City could look, I think, after a terrible disaster – or simply in the fullness of time.

The monsoon that beautifies and enriches the countryside had made Calcutta ugly and almost uninhabitable. Rain in India gives all buildings, especially modern ones, a peculiar look of senility. The streets were flooded, there were stalled cars everywhere, and people wading among the dead dogs, and the dampness had given the stucco a rather mouldy colour. It was impossible to tell whether a building had been put up a year ago or centuries ago – all brickwork becomes stained very quickly in Calcutta's miserable climate.

"Under prevailing conditions, Calcutta's future is very dark,'' Professor Chatterjee told me in Calcutta one afternoon. Professor Chatterjee was an astrologer. He then told me (after a brief examination of my palm) that I would live to the age of seventy-eight, have another child (a daughter) and be given problems by people of small size; I was sentimental, he said, which wasn't at all helpful, and when I was forty-four or forty-five I would – in his words – be very celebrated.

I found some of this reassuring. The part about small people was certainly true. It was a small man who refused to find me a bedroll, and another small man who demanded that I double his tip, and yet another who overcharged me in a taxi, and a fourth little man who insisted that I get in touch with his brother in California to settle some family litigation that was long overdue; and four small porters squabbled so furiously over carrying my suitcases that I ended up carrying them myself in order to keep the peace.

It was in Calcutta that I began to reflect on my travelling across the Sub-continent by train, going from station to station. The stations had everything – not only food and retiring rooms and human company, but also each station possessed the peculiar character of its city. There were disadvantages, though. The railway retiring rooms could be fairly awful – rats were common and there were often cows downstairs. The food was, I found, undistinguished. And there was often pandemonium at these stations. But it was in every respect the sedentary adventure I had expected.

THE KAMRUP EXPRESS TO NEW JALPAIGURI

I had wanted to take this train to Assam, to Nowgong and Silchar, and then to descend into Sylhet and move sideways into Bangladesh. But this was now impossible. There was fighting in Assam, civil strife between Assamese and Bengalis, and the Nagas had never really been pacified. If I needed proof of that I had only to look at the passengers on the Kamrup Express: they were men from the Indian Air Force and the Army; they had unfinished business in Assam.

Even New Jalpaiguri and Darjeeling are officially Disturbed Areas, and foreign travellers needed a special permit to visit these places. This permit is obtained in the crowded, littered Circumlocution Office in Calcutta, and when it is shown at the railway station in Jalpaiguri your passport is stamped, much as it would be if you were crossing into another country.

In most respects, the Kamrup Express was an ordinary – even somewhat disagreeable – train. But in India there is nothing remarkable about a train that is slow and dirty – particularly one that is making a long journey through such remote provinces. In one respect, the Kamrup Express was unusual: it had a dining car. For hours after we left, relays of men – only men – sat squashing rice and dal in their fists and flinging it into their mouths. Meanwhile, the kitchen staff boiled cauldrons of lentils and crouched between the cars peeling potatoes.

It had begun to rain. The kitchen fires were stoked again. The men were still eating, and lines of more men waited throughout the train to take their turn at the tables. In spite of the rain, it was very hot, and the fans in the dining car whirred and scraped. The rain was loud; so were the fans, so were the eaters. It was all motion and noise, and at midnight they were all still at it.

At dawn everything was different and serene. It was dry here, but the trees were green, and not far away were the dim blue shapes of mountains to the north and north-west. We were scheduled to arrive at 7.15. At 7.30 we stopped at a tiny station near the negligible village of Dhumdanj, which was no more than a few cows and a few families and one buffalo.

Two hours passed. This is an aspect of train travel that must not be overlooked: the unexplained stop in the middle of nowhere; and the unexplained delay – hours during which only a dog barks, and someone shuts off a radio, and a child emerges from the tall grass beside the track to sell tea in disposable clay cups. You don't know whether you will leave in two minutes or two days, so it is dangerous to stray very far from the train. The sun moves higher in the sky. A child begins to weep. Then an unexplained whistle and a few seconds later the train moves, and five hundred Indians run alongside, trying to board.

"There are landslides on the line," the policeman said at New Jalpaiguri as he stamped my passport and examined my permit. "You can't take the train to Darjeeling from here."

But I could take it farther on, beyond the damaged sections of track.

THE TOY TRAIN TO DARJEELING

When I was reading *Erewhon*, Samuel Butler's utopian novel, on this train I came across the sentence, "Exploring is delightful to look forward to and back upon, but it is not comfortable at the time, unless it be of such an easy nature as not to deserve the name." Peshawar in July had been scorching; Amritsar had been flooded, and Varanasi in August had been stinking and soggy. The other day I had been splashing through undrained and overheated Calcutta, and now on the way to wet and dark Darjeeling I was cold. So perhaps this was exploring after all and not merely a chug across the Sub-continent.

Everyone calls it the Toy Train. It is a narrow-gauge mountain railway, with the sort of small blue steam engines that other people put into transport museums. They are very old and very rusty, but still serviceable; the coaches are box-like and furnished rather austerely with wooden benches. It is one of the slowest railway journeys in the world – eight or ten kilometres per hour – and it can take twelve hours to go the seventy-six miles from New Jalpaiguri to Darjeeling.

On the face of it, it is a dreary run-down affair that most countries would have scrapped long ago. But a closer look reveals a real jewel, a tremendously ingenious piece of engineering – a true original. If it is inconvienient it is because in the hundred years in which it has been running it has never been improved and hardly been maintained. It was bravely built and it looks so clever and powerful that it seems an impertinence to do anything to it except ride it and let it run. It actually looks indestructible.

The engine is a model of practicality. Just enough room inside for the driver and the fireman; and the engine powerful enough for these steep grades. It is the most old-fashioned machine imaginable. There is a sandbox over the cow-catcher. I asked what it was for and was told that in wet weather when traction is poor the wheels slip, and then a man squats near the sandbox and throws handfuls of sand on the tracks, just in front of the wheels. There are often four or five men clambering over this engine as it climbs towards Darjeeling.

The tracks are also the road, like tramlines in an old American street; but on this railway line dogs sleep between the tracks, and children play on the tracks and roll toys along them, and the tracks are also put to practical use by men who push huge logs along them – just skidding them downhill on the rails.

The four coaches are nearly always full, if not with legitimate travellers then with joy riders – the train is part of the life of the long series of mountainsides that connect Siliguri to Darjeeling. Some people only ride a hundred yards, others are going miles. It is full of businessmen, farmers, Buddhist monks and schoolchildren. Every ticket is made out in duplicate, though none of them costs more than a few cents.

The train passes by the houses and it is inches away from the windows. It is almost as if the train is inside those houses. Could any machine be more familiar here? It passes close enough to the shops and stalls for a train passenger to reach out and pick an onion or an apple out of a basket on the shop counter. On my train a boy picked a flower as we passed the embankment and handed the flower to a woman in a shop – and he had not done much more than stretch out his hand. And there are flowers everywhere – blue hydrangeas, yellow evening primroses, and carnations and roses, all tangled across the hillsides next to the tracks, with the high ferns and the thickets of bamboo. And beyond all this lushness is the tea, great terraces of it on the steep mountainsides.

The valleys and these hillsides are open to the distant plains, and so the traveller on the toy train has a view which, like the one from the station at Sonada, seems almost unnatural it is so dramatic. It is like standing at the heights of a gigantic outdoor amphitheatre and looking down and seeing the plains and the rivers, roads and crops printed upon it and flattened by the yellow heat. There are wisps and whorls of cloud down there, too. Up here at Sonada it is dark green and wet and cold, like a different country, where nearly everyone has rosy cheeks.

After Sonada we came to Jor Bungalow Station and then Ghoom, the highest railway station in Asia at 7,407 feet (2,257 metres). The mist shifts slightly and farther along, towards Darjeeling, it is possible on a clear day to see the long irregular ridge of rock massively white in the great folds of snow-covered rock: Kanchenjunga.

The so-called "Ghoom Loop" is the famous descent in which the train appears to be tying itself into a knot while at the same time whistling to clear its own caboose out of the way, and after three or four curves it continues on its way, gliding into Darjeeling, still following the main road and bumping past the shops and sharing the thoroughfare with the Buddist monks and the bullock carts.

Darjeeling in unlike Simla. It is not an Indian resort but rather a Nepali town. It is a solemn place, full of schools and convents and monasteries. It is barer than Simla, not as populous; it is muddier, friendlier, very oriental looking and rather un-Indian in aspect. Simla has visitors, Darjeeling has residents; Simla is Anglo-Indian, but Darjeeling is Oriental. It is not posh. There is no society here – no Promenade, no Mall. It is the more relaxing for having no pretensions. And it is racially much more interesting because the various races have taken root and become resident – people from Nepal, Kashmir, China, Sikkim, Bhutan; and Tibetans, Bengalis and people from as far afield as Rajasthan and Bombay, who came here to escape the plains and just stayed. It is a hospitable place.

The curse of the town is its traffic – an endless procession of honking jeeps and trucks. In any case, the real horror of India is less what is seen than what is heard. It may be the noisiest country in the world: it is a terrible fate. And in Darjeeling where human life is jammed in the narrow valleys there is a constant jarring on the ear during the day-light hours. At night it is silent, for no one dares to drive on those dangerous roads in the darkness, and the trains don't run at night.

It seemed to me that most of Darjeeling's problems would probably be solved with a modern version of the train, which was finished just a hundred years ago. It was a great solution then, and it still serves the town, for many people commute from places like Ghoom to jobs in Darjeeling – to the shops, to the government offices, and even to the stranger occupations in Darjeeling such as the carver of yak bones and the clerk who stands under the sign "Licensed Vendor for Ganja & Bhang". Ten grams of ganja (marijuana) – 30 cents.

It badly needs to be improved, but of course the wonder of it – like the wonder of much else in India – is that it still operates. India is a vast and complex place. The phones seldom work, the mail is unreliable, the electricity is subject to sudden stoppages. There are numerous natural disasters and there are eight hundred million people. It seems almost inconceivable that this country is still viable, and yet there are times when one gets glimpses of its greatness. At first it is infuriating, but after a while, when one is better acquainted with its weaknesses, one marvels at the way it runs. Towards the end of my Indian journey I decided that India runs primarily because of the railway. It is an old-fashioned solution, but India has old-fashioned problems. It is impossible to imagine India without the railway, or to think what could conceivably replace it.

THE ULKA EXPRESS TO CHITTAGONG

This train was on the world news the day I took it: it was the only link between Dhaka and Chittagong – every other road was under five feet of water, and scores of people had drowned in the torrential rains. But the monsoon comes every year to Bangladesh, and every year it is bad. It is so predictably terrible it is not remarkable. It was not the major news item in the national newspaper, the *Bangladesh Observer*. This unfortunate country was just having another unlucky week.

Dhaka is an odd, low, featureless place of wide streets and mainly rickshaw traffic. In its apparent order is a kind of hopelessness and hunger: it looks as if it has submitted to the aid-givers' notions of how it should look. It seems a threadbare and cringing sort of place, not the loud futuristic folly that Calcutta is.

The Dhaka railway station, built after what Bangladeshis call Liberation, is big and airy and waterstained like every other building in the country. There are few trains in Bangladesh, and so it is not a busy station – not many travellers, not much life, very little to buy. When the train pulls out the station is empty. This is never the case in India, where the local railway station is treated like a community centre.

The refugees in Dhaka – what are they fleeing? perhaps natural disasters – seem rather dazed and stupified-looking, living in huts by the railway tracks. They live in low burlap-covered tents or straw huts, or on wobbly bamboo frames built on ponds of black water. In the morning, as the Ulka Express draws out, these scenes have a particular poignancy, with the people going through the motions of washing clothes, bathing, cooking, cleaning, brushing teeth – all in the filthiest water. Early morning in the tropical slum by the tracks reveals all its pathetic secrets.

It was not immediately obvious that the rain was a disaster. Today the sun was shining, and this whole southern part of Bangladesh had been turned into a spectacular lake – hundreds of miles of floodwater. And the only things showing in all that water were the long straight rails of the railway track.

The Ulka Express, fifteen coaches long – one was First class – was pulled by a diesel engine. I would have gone Second but I would not have got a seat, and I was not prepared to stand for nine hours.

At Tungi Junction I saw another train pull in. There were perhaps fifty people clinging to the sides of the engine and hanging from the carriages and sitting and standing on the coach roofs. These seemingly magnetized people had the effect of making the train look small. They completely covered it and of course the paying passengers were jammed inside.

It made me curious about seating arrangements on the Ulka Express. I leaned out of the window and saw that, apart from my coach, the whole train was exactly the same – people everywhere, holding on to the sides, the engine, and crowding the roofs.

To the sound of a younger beggar boy's flute, the train rattled south. It was the sort of bright sunny day that could only come after days of rain – the whole sky had been emptied onto this part of Bangladesh and now the sky was clear and blue and the land was under water.

At 9.00 a.m. we came to Narsingdi Junction, and the train was besieged by beggars – many lame and blind, but many more in apparently good health as they demanded money. It is impossible to recall travelling in Bangladesh without hearing the incessant cry "Baksheesh!" – "Boksis!" in the local pronunciation. For this reason, and also because of the mobs, I came to dread the stations – each was worse than the last.

In the hot, stricken country the only thing that moved was the railway. But there was no panic. At Akhaura ("Change Here for Sylhet") a man stood up to his waist in a flooded field serenely washing his cow, and farther on boats had penetrated to villages – the large boats were beamy, like old Portuguese frigates, and the smaller ones were gracefully shaped like Persian slippers.

"You will see where President Zia was assassinated in Chittagong," Mr. Shahid said as we rolled along. It was as if he was passing on a piece of tourist information. He did say that I should have taken the Karnafuli Express – it did not stop often and therefore there were fewer people clinging to its sides.

At Comilla I met a young man who had just opened an office to encourage Bangladeshis to enroll in a Voluntary Sterilization programme.

"Some people come forward," he said. "But not enough. We have to motivate them. They need incentives..."

What sort? I wondered.

"We have tried money and clothes as a sort of reward, but it is not enough. We need something more substantial. There is no problem with middle-class people. I have two children myself and I think that is a good number. The problem is with the poor. But this is a democratic country, and so we do not make sterilization compulsory."

Was he making any progress?

"Very slow progress," he said.

The worst of the floods were south of Comilla, at the town of Feni. But there was no visible distress, only a kind of gloomy resignation – people resolutely baling out their houses and fields, but just as many taking baths. The children in the area were swimming and diving and having a great time. The floods had also brought fish to these hungry people, and where the banks of rivers had been breached people were enthusiastically fishing with nets, scoops, lines, buckets and ancient-looking fish traps.

The day continued hot, but the flood did not abate. Now the heat was intolerable, and under the cloudless sky there was an endless flood. Chittagong lay just ahead, simmering under the sun. It is not a prepossessing town. It is a rotting settlement on the estuary of the Karnafuli River – it is docks, mouldy buildings, prowling seamen, blackened palm trees and storm-damaged roads. The airport had been closed for five days. It too was underwater. Even the people in Chittagong admit there is very little to see there. They say, "Go to Rangamati" (colourful tribesmen), "See Karnafuli Reservoir" (a big lake), or "Go to Cox's Bazaar" (a seedy resort farther down the Bay of Bengal). I did not make any more plans. For me this was the end of the imperial way.

PAKISTAN

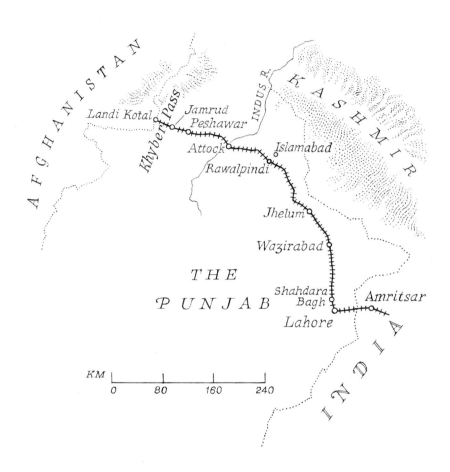

AFGHANISTAN

Landi Kotal   Khyber Pass   Jamrud
                              Peshawar
                    Attock   Islamabad
                 Rawalpindi

INDUS R.

KASHMIR

Jhelum

Wazirabad

THE

PUNJAB

Shahdara   Amritsar
Bagh
Lahore

INDIA

KM
0   80   160   240

Dwarfed by nature,
this sixty-year-old veteran leads its train
along a precarious ledge
into a tunnel in the Khyber Pass.
Its brother assists at the rear.

Medicine man
selling herbs by the main station.
Peshawar.
(Above) "The beaky, craggy faces
of the travellers ..."
A Pathan in Peshawar.

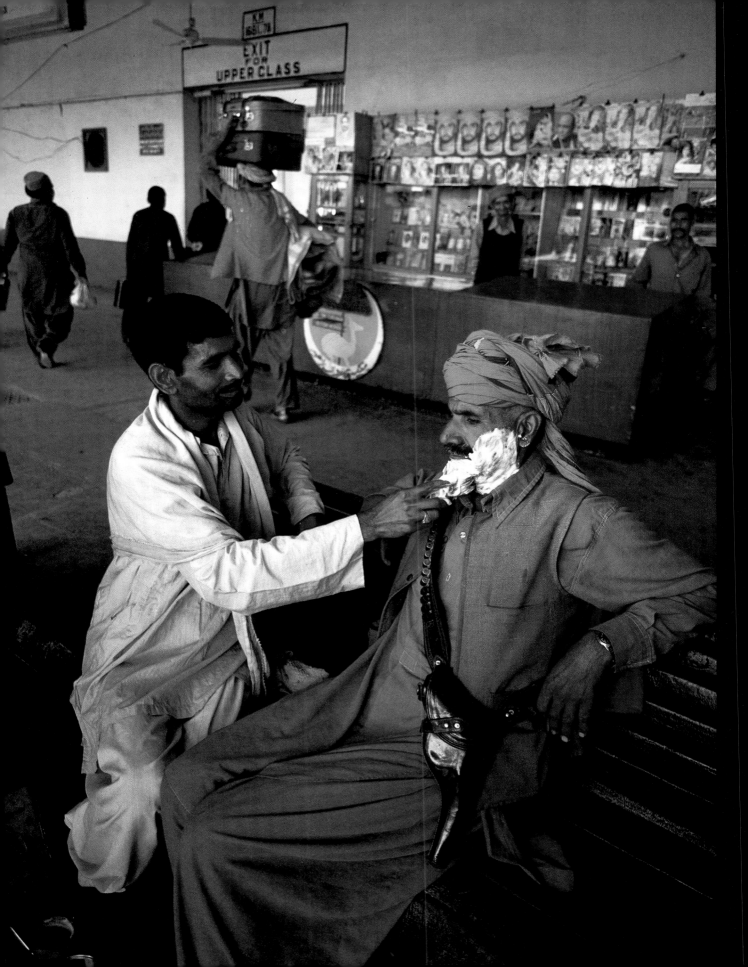

At *Peshawar Cantonment Station,*
Superintendent Abbas Ali Shah's pride in its cleanliness
is reflected in his own attire.
(Opposite) "The people were always dressed like this,
and always armed . . ."
Time for a leisurely shave at Peshawar.

Armed now with the tools
of his trade, this Pathan "lengthsman" is one of hundreds
who patrol and maintain the track through the Khyber Pass.
(Opposite) *The solution to one waiter's shortage of tea.*

Fresh *fruit for the hot*
and dusty hours ahead.
(Opposite) *The Quissa Khawani Bazaar, Peshawar.*

Ringing bell to signal
arrival of trains. Rawalpindi.
(Opposite) *Still bearing its pre-Partition classification,
SG/S 2400 and its driver await the starting signal
for yet another journey. Nourshera.*

Time to face Mecca
for the evening prayers.
(Above) Face lift
for a peeling façade.
Poster painting
is one of the most
highly-developed
visual art-forms
in the sub-continent.
Rawalpindi.

Patience; the train will come.

(Above) *"Pakistan was more Islamic ..."*
Women wearing "borquas" to observe purdah. Rawalpindi.

INDIA

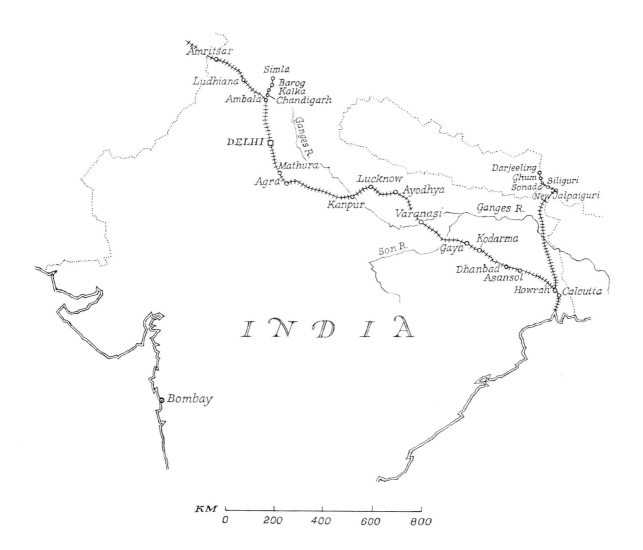

Bengali woman and child
look out of the window at the vast Indian landscape.
(Overleaf) "Part of the land, as natural
as a gully or a hill . . ."
The narrow-gauge line climbs inexorably
towards Simla.

*L*ocal stone
and man's artistry
combine to bridge
one of the many gaps
confronting the builders
of the Kalka-Simla Railway.

New Delhi Station:
a bookseller looks forward to a brisk day's business
in new titles; sunglasses for the men,
necklaces for the women, and combs for both.
(Opposite) Traditional dress and modern luggage.
A Punjabi woman awaits a safe path across the tracks.

People travelling on a "People's Express"
are advised to be patient because service often runs hours late.
Such Janata trains offer only basic second class.
(Opposite) Second-class passengers cram themselves
and their belongings onto the Assam Mail.

Old *Delhi Railway Station*
– early morning.

The *"Desert Queen"*
at night.

Lizards being sold
as aphrodisiacs. Old Delhi Station.

Departure.
Indian woman with sari and fashionably large tika.
(Opposite) *This passenger
makes good use of her bed-roll
while awaiting her train at New Delhi Station.*

Second class. Lucknow.
(Opposite) *"The Great Indian Rover"*
tours centres of Buddhist pilgrimage,
accompanied by a garlanded Buddha
who presides over the Club Car.

Immaculate staff
prepare culinary delights
in the modern kitchen car
of "The Great Indian Rover".

A *restorative cup of tea.*
(Opposite) *Washing facilities are not quite
as they would be in the West.*
(Overleaf) *The sun sets over Agra Fort Station
as carriages are watered and given a routine inspection.
In the background, Jama Marjid Mosque.*

Undistracted by the splendour
of the Taj Mahal,
    a Permanent-way Inspector
gives his full attention to his track.

Line inspector pushed by retinue
during check for wear and tear on tracks. Agra.
(Overleaf) *A morning train rumbles across the bridge
into Agra while men and women beat the dirt and the life
out of garments in the waters of the Yamuna river below.*
(Opposite) *Outside the Taj Mahal.*

*V*aranasi Station, where the cows
regard passengers as interlopers.
(Opposite) *It's cooler here than in the kitchen
of "The Great Indian Rover".*

Ubiquitous *platform
vendors supply fruit, nuts,
tea and fizzy drinks to sustain life
till the next halt.*
(Above) *Wayside bargaining at Lucknow.*

Ayodhya:
Monkeys are associated
with the Hindu
monkey-god, Hanuman.
(Right) A sadhu (holy man)
gives advice and a blessing,
in exchange for
a little baksheesh.
(Opposite) One solution
to the litter problem –
banana skins are handed
to the sacred monkeys.

One face of India.
Second-class, Varanasi
(Opposite) *Villager smoking* bedi,
Indian cigarette. Varanasi.

Villagers strap bicycles
to outside of train to save time
getting on and off. Varanasi.
(Opposite) Improvisation. Journey to market;
the milk keeps cool
and leaves more room for the passengers.

89

Resignation
on the faces of a farmer
and his son
as a pet goat is taken
on a local train to market.

This passenger in a second-class
2-tier compartment near Calcutta.

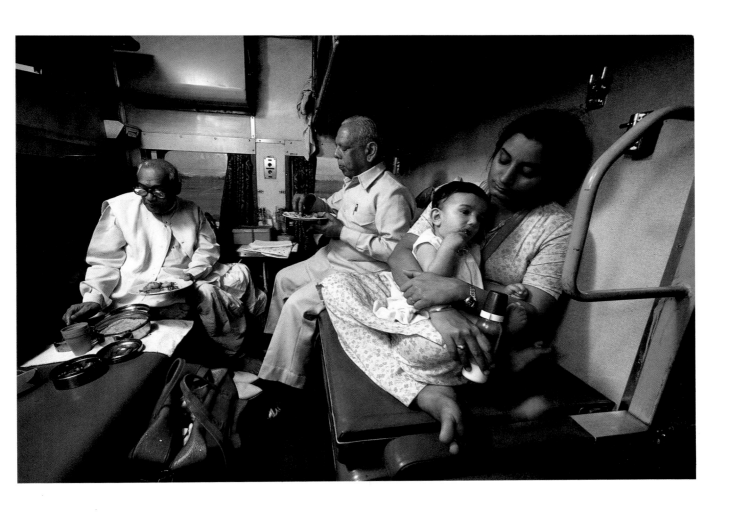

Modern second-class
air-conditioned sleeping car
with a family enjoying their traditional meal.
Varanasi to Calcutta train.

A *shaft of sunlight*
pierces the gloom
of Calcutta's Howrah Station.
(Above) First-class passenger's restaurant.
Calcutta.

Howrah Station, Calcutta.
Inside one of the several signal boxes
which control the traffic.
(Opposite) *Before the present Howrah Bridge,*
from which this view was taken, was built,
a bridge-of-boats spanned the river in front of the station
to connect it with Calcutta.
(Overleaf) *The concourse: "Enormous and noisy,*
a combination of grandeur and desolation . . .",
built as the terminus of the erstwhile East Indian Railway.

Electric suburban services operate
from Howrah and battle with the intensive rush-hour traffic.
Under less crowded conditions,
travelling shoe-shine boys ply their trade.
(Opposite) The narrow-gauge branch lines
provide a useful, if unremunerative service.
Men taking their hay to market near Calcutta.

The "Toy Train"
to Darjeeling.

Darjeeling: *"The engine is a model
of practicality . . . There are often four or five men
clambering over the engine . . ."*
Sand for the rails is in the box in the front;
men to apply it perch on either side.

Darjeeling:
*Smiling, immaculate Nepalese schoolgirls
share the road with the train; the boys have jumped aboard.
(Opposite) ". . . dogs sleep between the tracks . . ."
(Overleaf) The town, clinging to the slopes
of the Himalayan foothills
with a background of snow-clad peaks
and Kanchenjunga dominating the scene.*

D*arjeeling:*
scenes along the tracks (pages 110–17)

BANGLADESH

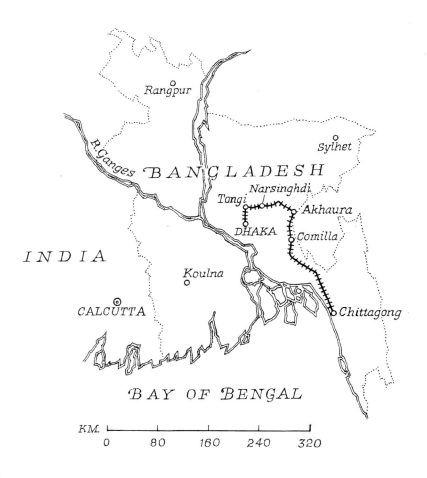

Rangpur

R. Ganges

BANGLADESH

Sylhet

Narsinghdi

Tongi · · · · Akhaura

DHAKA · Comilla

INDIA

Koulna

CALCUTTA

Chittagong

BAY OF BENGAL

KM.
0   80   160   240   320

(Overleaf) *Overgrown tracks give way
to the road as cycle-rickshaws
invade the railway yard. Dhaka.*

F*aces.*

(Overleaf) *Built to remain above the annual inundation,*
the tracks are often occupied by entire villages,
camping till the floods subside.

R*esignation*
and contemplation.

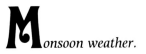

Monsoon weather.

"The children
in the area were swimming
and diving
and having a wonderful time..."
On the Dhaka-Chittagong line.

(Overleaf) *The effects of the monsoon.*

A *cowherd resting on the tracks*
because it is the driest ground in the monsoon flooding.
The once-a-day train passed through in the morning.

*C*hittagong:
Night falls
on a soggy station yard
as a train weaves it way
from the left
onto the main line.

Special thanks to Bill Garrett,
editor of the National Geographic magazine,
who made this train trip possible.
And many thanks to Tom Smith, Bob Gilka and Elie Rogers
for their support all along the way.

Steve McCurry